search for the
golden moon bear

search for the
golden moon bear

science and adventure in the asian tropics

by Sy Montgomery

HOUGHTON MIFFLIN COMPANY   BOSTON 2004

In memory of Ruthie Weber Galbreath and Don H. Galbreath,
with thanks for raising a great scientist.

www.houghtonmifflinbooks.com

Book design by Lisa Diercks
The text of this book
is set in Manticore.

*Library of Congress Cataloging-in-Publication
Data*

Montgomery, Sy.
  Search for the golden moon bear : sci-
ence and adventure in the Asian
tropics / by Sy Montgomery.
    p. cm.
  Adaptation of: Search for the golden
moon bear. New York : Simon &
Schuster, c2002.
  ISBN 0-618-35650-9
  1. Asiatic black bear—Asia, Southeast-
ern—Juvenile literature. 2. Scientific
expeditions—Asia, Southeastern—
Juvenile literature. I. Montgomery, Sy.
Search for the golden moon bear. II.
Title.
  QL737.C27M654 2004
  599.78—dc22

2004005236

Printed in Singapore
TWP 10 9 8 7 6 5 4 3 2 1

Photo Credits
GARY GALBREATH: pp. 4, 6, 18 (bottom), 20, 21 (bottom), 28, 30, 31, 36 (left), 41, 44, 47 (top), 49, 50 (top), 52, 54, 55 (top), 56, 67 (bottom), 70 (bottom), 75 (bottom). SY MONTGOMERY: pp. 1, 8, 9, 10 (top), 16, 17, 18 (top), 19, 22, 24, 26 (top), 29, 34, 35 (top), 37, 38, 42, 51, 67 (top), 72, 73, 74 (bottom), 76, 78, 79 (left). JOE PALLEN: pp. 58, 59, 61, 62, 64, 65. ALAN RABINOWITZ: pp. 32 (top), 33 (right). DIANNE TAYLOR-SNOW: cover, pp. 2, 11 (bottom right), 15 (right), 21 (top), 36 (right), 43, 46, 48 (bottom), 55 (bottom), 66, 70 (top), 71, 74 (top), 75 (top), 77, 80 (top). GEORGE SCHALLER: pp. 26 (bottom), 32 (bottom), 33 (left). V.U.: pp. 23, 39. ART WOLFE: pp. 11 (bottom left and top right), 12 (top), 14, 35 (bottom), 40, 69. HENG KIMCHHAY: p. 80 (bottom left). DR. PENNY WALKER: p. 10 (bottom). DAVE WELLING: pp. 27, 48 (top). JAMES P. ROWAN: pp. 13, 15 (left), 68. MINDEN PICTURES: pp. 11 (top left), 12 (bottom), 47 (middle), 57. STEVE INGRAM: p. 47 (bottom). GARY VAN ZUYLAN: p. 79 (right).

Cover photo by Dianne Taylor-Snow.
Illustrations on pp. 5, 60, and 63 by Liddy Hubbell.
Illustration of bear on chapter openers and jacket flap by Gabrielle Cosel.

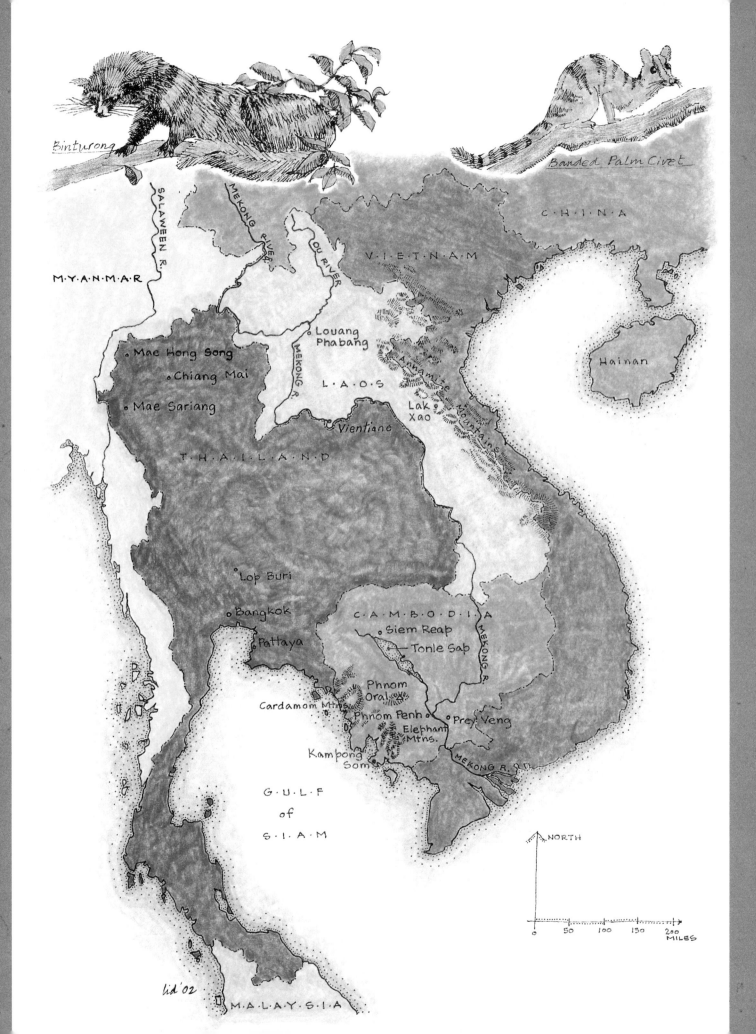

Binturong

Banded Palm Civet

C·H·I·N·A

MYANMAR

SALAWEEN R.

MEKONG RIVER

OU RIVER

V·I·E·T·N·A·M

MEKONG R.

Louang Phabang

Mae Hong Song

Chiang Mai

L·A·O·S

Annamite Mountains

Hainan

Mae Sariang

Lak Xao

Vientiane

T·H·A·I·L·A·N·D

Lop Buri

Bangkok

C·A·M·B·O·D·I·A

Siem Reap

MEKONG R.

Pattaya

Tonle Sap

Phnom Oral

Cardamom Mtns.

Phnom Penh

Prey Veng

Elephant Mtns.

Kampong Som

MEKONG R.

G·U·L·F
of
S·I·A·M

NORTH

0   50   100   150   200
MILES

lid '02

M·A·L·A·Y·S·I·A

three
beginnings

From the leafy shadows of the little outdoor cage, a pale face stared out at us — the face of a shy, young female bear.

The sight of her took our breath away. She was as unusual as she was beautiful. Framed by the cream-colored fur of her face, her brown eyes were ringed in black, almost like a panda's. But she was no panda. Her ears were big and round, and stood up like those on Mickey Mouse. She had a furry mane, like an adult male lion's. On her chest was a white V, like on a college sweater. But what was most exciting was her amazing color. The fur of her back, sides, and belly — most of the bear, in fact — was different shades of gold. She was like no other bear we'd seen before, not even in a photo or on television.

What kind of bear was she? We had come a long way to meet her—all the way to Cambodia in Southeast Asia. But with good reason. As we sweated in the jungly heat, we realized with awe that we were looking at a bear that was unknown to science.

But wait—haven't all the animals in the world been discovered already? Far from it!

Scientists are discovering new creatures all the time. From the tall canopies of rainforest trees to the depths of oceans, new insects and unknown fish are uncovered every year. Occasionally someone finds a new species of frog or rat or bird.

But this was a new bear—a big mammal! How could it be that no scientist had seen it before? Could we find others like her? Did they all live in one area, or were they all over Southeast Asia? And what, exactly, was this bear? Was this an entirely new species? Was it a new color of a species already known? Or was the light coat simply one the young bear would outgrow?

That's what we came to find out.

This is the story of our scientific search. It's a story full of surprises. Our discovery didn't happen the way you might expect. What we actually found out was very different from what we'd originally imagined—and important for different reasons than we had thought. In fact, just about everything about our search for the golden moon bear was surprising, right from the beginning.

Or maybe I should say "beginnings"—because this story has not just one beginning, but three: one in the tropical province of Yunnan, China; one in the Peruvian Amazon; and one in my small hometown in southern New Hampshire. For one of our surprises was that sometimes, discovery is waiting for you just around the corner. And sometimes it takes you around the world.

"We were in this little town in Yunnan called Simao," the scientist told me as we canoed down the dark waters of a tributary of the Amazon one night in June. Dr. Gary Galbreath, an evolutionary biologist and professor at Northwestern University, was always telling me cool stories. He told me about the armadillos he had studied in Florida as a grad-

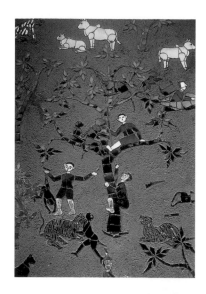

TOP: Buddhist temple mosaic, made of tiny tiles and mirrors.
BOTTOM: Carvings on temple door.

uate student (a pair of them used to sleep with him in his bed). He told me about giant sabre-toothed cats, American zebras, and giant ground sloths—creatures whose fossils he had sorted at Chicago's famous Field Museum of Natural History. He told me about the giant carnivorous terror birds —wingless, six-foot-tall birds who seized their prey in two-fingered hands—who used to haunt the Amazon during the Age of Mammals. I was writing a book on the Amazon, so I always listened to him carefully.

Dr. Gary Galbreath, evolutionary biologist, in front of a mural at a Buddhist temple.

But on this particular night, Gary was telling me about his first trip to a very different land—China. He had traveled there in 1988 with a group of other biologists. While visiting a little town in Yunnan, China's most tropical province, he saw something that he would never forget.

"My friend Penny called me over," he told me. "She said there was some-

This ancient Cambodian temple at Angkor is so old that a huge fig tree is now growing around its stones.

thing I should see. And there, in this little cage—it was sort of like a town mascot, and taking peanuts, very gently, from people's hands—was this young male bear with tall, round ears and a white V on the chest. But what was remarkable was, its coat was golden. I had never seen anything like it."

Neither had any other scientist, Gary soon discovered. He visited China's great natural history museum, at Kunming, and looked through its collection of bear skins. Not one looked anything like the bear he'd seen! When he got back to the United States, he searched through scientific papers about bears. He even translated papers written in other languages. No scientist had ever described a bear like this!

"I always wanted to go back there and find out more," Gary told me. But China is a long way to go. Would the bear still be there? Even if it was, this was just one specimen. That's not enough to prove you've discovered a new species or even a new color. What if the gold bear were just a single weirdo, like a five-legged cow?

Still, Gary never forgot that bear. Here we were, nearly ten years later, and he was still wondering about it. "But it was just one weird bear," Gary told me that night in the Amazon. "Surely if it were something new, it would have already been discovered. . . ."

Or so we thought—until a year later, when I met Sun Hean.

This time I was back home in New Hampshire. I was going to a friend's birthday party, about three miles from my house. There I met a young man who was visiting one of the guests at the party. Sun Hean was one of the youngest people in the room—he wasn't even thirty years old yet. He knew no one else there. He was shy. But I was eager to talk with him. Sun Hean was from Cambodia—a tropical land in Southeast Asia—and I wanted to hear all about its jungle animals.

I knew about Cambodia's wild Asian elephants, and Indochinese tigers, and two kinds of bears—sun bears and moon bears, both of them jet black. I remembered Gary's golden bear. "In your country," I asked Sun Hean, "have you ever heard of a bear that *wasn't* black?"

The young man's brown eyes grew wide with astonishment. Why, yes

Gary Galbreath met his first golden mystery bear in Yunnan, China, more than fifteen years ago.

LEFT TO RIGHT:
Sun bear, with its tiny ears and short fur; Asian elephants; Indochinese tigers; moon bear.

—in fact, he had just received photographs from one of his coworkers in Cambodia of a very interesting bear, a very strange and beautiful bear, he told me. She had been caught wild and was now living in a cage on a palm plantation in southwestern Cambodia.

"What does it look like?" I asked.

Sun Hean replied, "It is the color of gold . . ."

A few weeks later, I arranged for Sun Hean and Gary to meet. The two men compared photographs of the two golden bears, taken one thousand kilometers and eleven years apart. They were nearly identical. Now it wasn't just one weird bear. We knew there were more out there. But what *were* they?

We began to plan our expedition.

"Nearly everywhere there have been bears," Gary says, "people have argued over how many different types there are." Even scientists get confused trying to sort out bear colors and bear species. Sometimes the species called the black bear is white—and sometimes the species called the brown bear is black! Here's a rundown on the different species of bears known when we set out on our mission in 1999. See if you can keep them straight.

North American Black Bear

(*Ursus americanus*): This is the bear you're most likely to meet at home. These big bears can weigh up to 600 pounds and are more common than you might think. In some parts of the American East Coast, black bears sometimes den under suburban houses and have been known to steal cooling pies off back porches! Happily, this is a gentle giant. Plants make up 80 percent of its diet. It seldom kills anything bigger than a mouse. In the eastern United States, the black bear almost never attacks people. Black bears who see people in the woods usually climb a tree to escape. But some people encountering these bears in the open say they've heard bears call out in alarm—in a voice almost like a person's! This is a wonderful bear, but it doesn't have a very good name. Black bears are often black, but they can also be brown, blond, or even white. The white ones are sometimes called "spirit bears" because they are revered by native people in coastal British Columbia in Canada, where they are found. DNA studies show that these beautiful white bears are the same species as the other American "black" bears—and the brown-colored "black bears" are, too.

Grizzly Bear, a.k.a. Brown Bear

(*Ursus arctos*): Everyone knows about America's grizzlies—the big, strong, hump-shouldered bears of Yellowstone fame. They were so feared that scientists gave them the Latin name *Ursus arctos horribilis*. *Ursus* means bear; *arctos* means north; and you can guess what *horribilis* means! The American grizzly has three names, showing it's a *subspecies* of what some scientists call the brown bear. Unlike separate species, members of different subspecies can mate and produce healthy offspring—but they generally don't because they're usually separated by some boundary, like mountains, a river, or an ocean. Scientists are still arguing over how many different kinds or subspecies of brown bear there are—possibly more than eighty! But because "brown" bears can be almost any color, Gary prefers to call them all grizzlies. On the Indian subcontinent, there is a so-called red bear or Himalayan grizzly (also known as the Isabelline bear—just to make things more confusing) that can be reddish, brown, yellow, or even white. There's another grizzly on the Tibetan plateau, called a blue bear, that isn't really blue but grayish black with a blond face. And there are subspecies of grizzlies of all different shapes, sizes, and lifestyles in between: a dwarf grizzly survives in Mongolia's Gobi Desert. Giant, ten-foot-long grizzlies patrol the cold forests of far eastern Russia. As huge an area as grizzlies now inhabit, their range used to be even larger. Before guns were invented, brown bears were common over most of Europe, including England, as well as west to the Mediterranean and east to the Pacific.

Polar Bear (*Ursus maritimus*): This white bear is the largest and most meat-loving bear on the planet. Living at the top of the world, it can stand 11 feet tall and weigh as much as 1,300 pounds.

It's strong enough to kill an 1,100-pound walrus or even a young beluga whale. Its stomach is big enough to hold 150 pounds of food! Polar bears are wonderful swimmers. They can swim 60 miles without resting, and have been found 200 miles offshore. That's why scientists named it *Ursus maritimus,* or the seafaring bear. Ironically, the white bear is really black. Its hair only looks white. The hairs, which are hollow to keep it warm, are actually colorless; beneath the colorless hair, the bear's skin is black. And here's another twist: DNA analysis shows that this white bear's closest living relatives are coal-black grizzly bears who today live on

Admiralty Island. These studies show the polar bear is a very young species—only half a million years old.

Spectacled Bear (*Tremarctos ornatus*): This South American bear got its name because the light rings around the eyes make it look like it's wearing glasses. A native of the highlands of the Andes ranges, it has shaggy fur and a short face. It represents an ancient branch of the bear family. Its first name—*Tremarctos*—shows it is different from most other bears. *Tremarctos* (think "tremble" + "arctic") means "fearsome northerner." A close relative of the spectacled

bear was the extinct giant short-faced bear, the largest meat-eating mammal that ever walked the earth. And it didn't just walk, it ran! Faster than a grizzly, more ferocious than a cave lion, the giant short-faced bear raced after North America's Pleistocene

zebras, bison, and camels and brought them down with a bite from canines larger than a leopard's. But this ferocious bear's surviving relative is a shy, gentle, rather small bear, usually weighing 175 to 275 pounds. It even looks somewhat scholarly, ornamented ("ornatus") with its "spectacles." The mother and cubs talk together by making a trilling sound. As humans cut into the highland forests of South America to make way for farms, spectacled bears are criti-

cally endangered, with perhaps only 2,000 of them left in the wild. Conservationists fear the spectacled bear could soon join its giant relative in extinction.

Panda (*Ailuropoda melanoleuca*): The cute black-and-white panda lives only in small areas along the east-ern rim of the Tibetan plateau in China. It's so different from other bears that it's the only bear in its genus: its Latin name means "the black-and-white (*melanoleuca*) cat-footed one (*Ailuropoda*)." Scientists argued for decades over whether it was really a bear or a relative of the raccoon. Though the Chinese had known about pandas for at least 3,000 years, and Western scientists had specimens of dead ones, no West-ern scientist ever saw a living panda until 1936, when a so-cialite widow, Ruth Harkness, brought the first live panda from China to Chicago. Everyone was spellbound. This adorable crea-ture seemed most un-bearlike.

Pandas eat almost nothing but bamboo. They don't roar, but bleat almost like a goat. Even though pandas live in the cool north, they don't hibernate. And unlike other bears, pandas don't have five fingers but six. The sixth finger works like a thumb, the better to hold bamboo (as it sits upright like a person at the dinner table). And that's a good thing, because the panda needs some forty-five pounds of bamboo stems and leaves a day to survive.

Sloth Bear (*Melursus ursinus*): With masses of fluffy, messy

black hair, the sloth bear sometimes ambles about, mumbling to itself like some absentminded professor. The messy hair comes in handy: baby bears ride the mother's back, hanging on to her coat like a subway rider clings to a strap on a train. The sloth bear was so named because people believed (wrongly) that it hung upside down from trees like a sloth. (In fact, at first scientists gave it the Latin name *Bradypus ursinus*—the bearlike sloth.) But it does something even more unlikely: with long claws, it digs a hole in tall termite mounds, then claps its flexible lips onto the hole and sucks the termites out, like a vacuum hose! It can also slam its nostrils shut so escaping termites can't crawl in.

Sun Bear (*Ursus malayanus*): The smallest and most tree-loving of bears looks more like a dog than a bear. And in fact, in some parts of Asia where people keep sun bears as pets, you might see one walking on a

leash just like a dog. The sun bear got its name because it often sports a sunrise-orange patch on the chest—very pretty against its velvety jet-black fur. You'd hardly notice the small ears. If you met a sun bear in Asia's tropical rainforests, you'd probably take note of its very long claws and stout, pointy canine teeth. But these aren't to hurt you: the claws help this bear climb trees, and the teeth help it open hard-shelled foods like coconuts.

Moon Bear (*Ursus thibetanus*): Its original Latin name, *Selenarctos thibetanus,* honored the Greek goddess of the moon, Selene. The crescent-moon-shaped patch of white on the chest shines like a moon on a dark night against the jet-black fur of the rest of its body. (Now the moon bear is

classed in the same group as most other bears, *Ursus.*) *Thibetanus* referred to Tibet, where the bear was first discovered in the snowy Himalayas. But this big, shaggy bear with the bushy mane also lives in many other parts of Asia, from Japan to China to Iran and Afghanistan. They don't look like they belong in the tropics, and in fact scientists didn't know they lived in Cambodia until the 1960s. Moon bears are smart and often appear in circuses and traveling shows, sometimes riding bicycles or skating on roller skates. They have been taught to walk upright like a person for a quarter of a mile!

FACING: Sun Hean prays at a temple.
TOP: Offerings of sweet incense left at a Buddhist temple.
BOTTOM: A monk sculpts an image of the Buddha.

science and species

So it was decided: we would leave for Cambodia in June, as soon as Gary finished teaching his spring classes.

Gary would be the senior scientist on the expedition. Now a silver-haired professor, Gary had wanted to be a scientist ever since he was a little boy collecting plastic dinosaurs (which he still has — plus some new ones that glow in the dark). He was always asking questions and trying to come up with answers: Why did the west coast of the African continent look like a puzzle piece that fit against the east coast of South America? How come birds reminded him so much of dinosaurs? Gary loves mysteries of all kinds — from detective stories (one of his favorite heroes is Sherlock Holmes) to algebra (because this kind of math is about

A road leads to the handmade homes of native people who still live in traditional ways.

solving for the unknown in an equation). He would be just the right person to direct how to solve the scientific mystery: Just what *was* this new bear?

Sun Hean would be in charge of getting us to our destinations in Cambodia. Though he was studying for his master's degree in wildlife studies in America, his real home was still Cambodia (where a person's first name is like his last name here, and vice versa—a situation so confusing we always called him by both names). Growing up on a small rice farm, Sun Hean had always dreamed of making lots of money. But instead he fell in love with Cambodia's native wildlife. He has devoted his life to protecting it. "Conservation can't make you rich," he told us, "but I don't care about that now." By the time Gary and I met him, Sun Hean was assistant director of Cambodia's brand-new Wildlife Protection Office. Sun Hean knew where to go, how to get there, and of course he could speak the national language of Cambodia, Khmer. We couldn't have asked for a better logistical coordinator.

And then there was me. I'm a writer, not a scientist. I'd never seen a golden bear. I'd never been to Cambodia. I would write a book about our expedition. But what would be *my* contribution to science?

I volunteered to stick my hands into a cage with a live bear in it—and pull out some of its hair with my eyebrow tweezers.

"Why do we need the hair?" Sun Hean asked.

This was how we'd find out what the golden bear was, Gary explained.

Sometimes you can tell right away if an animal is a whole new species. When the panda was discovered in China over a hundred years ago, it looked so different from any animal anyone had ever seen before, scientists argued for a century over whether it was a new kind of bear or a never-before-discovered relative of the raccoon! (It turned out to be a bear after all.) But sometimes it's not so easy. Take the eclectus parrot of Australia: the female is bright red and the male is bright green—but both are the same species.

"So how can scientists ever tell species apart?" Sun Hean asked Gary.

The biologist explained: "Animals of the same species generally look pretty much alike—but this isn't the only way you can tell. They also live

People leave flowers and food as offerings at shrines and spirit houses.

in the wild in the same place at the same time, and can breed with one another to produce healthy babies."

Scientists trying to classify new species sometimes make funny mistakes. Early explorers at the South Pole thought sleek adult King penguins and their fluffy brown chicks were different species—naming the babies the "woolly penguin." But today researchers have a new tool to help them tell species apart: DNA. And that's why I would need to pluck out bear hair.

"DNA is the stuff you inherit from your parents that makes you look like them—and causes members of the same species to look like each other," Gary explained. To find out if the golden bear was a new species or a new color of a known species, we would need to compare its DNA with those of other bears living in the same area.

DNA is present in every cell, but most often scientists take it from blood, bone, or the mass of cells called the *bulb* at the base of a hair. We didn't want to hurt the bears. So pulling out some of their hair was definitely the answer.

And I was the right person for the job. The only woman on the team, I had the smallest hands. My fingers were quick from years of playing piano and doing embroidery (my first Girl Scout badge was for needlework). I was happy to pluck bear hairs for science. Unfortunately, I was pretty sure the bears weren't going to like it.

How do you remove hairs from a bear without annoying the bear so much, it removes part of *you*? I gave this quite a bit of thought. Finally I came up with a plan. I made a packing list for the trip: long pants and rain poncho, insect repellent and sunscreen, snakeproof boots and sweat-absorbing socks, sun hat, water bottle, notebooks, pens, tape recorder, tweezers. . . .

And then I added a few other items you wouldn't normally tuck into your luggage: a huge bag of marshmallows and a few cans of sweetened condensed milk.

These weren't snacks for us. But like people, every bear has a sweet tooth. (The part about Winnie-the-Pooh's loving honey is true of real bears, too.) You get the idea: the sweet treats, I hoped, would keep the bear's mouth too busy to bite me while I plucked out its hairs!

We found that water buffalo, like bears, can come in different colors—sometimes even white!

But biting bears might be the least of our problems. Cambodia is a beautiful land, where people tend their emerald-colored rice fields in the old way, with the help of their patient water buffalo. It is a land of golden temples, wise monks, and great learning. Most Cambodians are Buddhists, following a philosophy that teaches peace and gentleness to all creatures. But Cambodia is also a country of sorrow and danger.

Sun Hean explained Cambodia's recent history to us. After the bloodshed of the Vietnam War more than thirty years ago, Cambodia suffered terribly under the rule of the Communist Khmer Rouge. ("Khmer" is the name of Cambodia's language and people; "Rouge" means red in French —a language widely spoken when Cambodia was under French rule. But the "Rouge" in Khmer Rouge always made Sun Hean think of blood.) Under the vicious Khmer Rouge leader, Pol Pot, more than a million people starved, died of disease, or were murdered as political enemies. To prevent people from escaping, the Khmer Rouge planted thousands of land mines in the earth. Many of these mines still hide, unexploded—waiting for someone to step on them. It happens all too often. Because of all the land mines, one in 236 Cambodians is missing a hand or a foot, a leg or an arm.

Pol Pot was overthrown in 1979, but his guerrillas continued to terrorize people. Until quite recently, Khmer Rouge terrorists particularly liked to kidnap Western visitors.

When we were planning our expedition in 1999, though, Sun Hean told us that the Cambodian government had the terrorists under control. But we might face a different problem: bandits. In fact, one travel book we read said bandits were so common that we'd better learn some Khmer so we could talk with them. It even offered a handy sentence for us to memorize: "That's a very nice gun, sir. I'd be honored to give you the gift of my truck."

On the other hand, Sun Hean said, there's a good side to almost everything. A good side to war, terrorism, and banditry? "The Khmer Rouge

Stone carvings at a temple in Cambodia's former capital, Angkor.

helped our country to protect animals," he said. Sun Hean was only half-joking. The terrorists were no animal lovers. But between the war and the land mines, the Khmer Rouge and the outlaws, for about thirty years few foreigners visited Cambodia. No one came to offer local people big money to cut down all their trees for timber or buy their exotic animals for trophies or exotic dinners.

Surprising though it may seem, the decades of human violence actually protected a hidden Eden in Cambodia. Forest still covers 60 percent of the country—the largest stretch of natural forest in mainland Southeast Asia. People stayed away from the land-mined mountain forests along Cambodia's borders with Thailand and Vietnam as well. Even scientists were afraid to go there for decades.

But when the first brave biologists finally started to trickle back to explore the forests again in the 1990s, they were in for some wonderful surprises.

The first was a 200-pound antelope with spearlike horns completely unknown to science. Then a giant barking deer with fangs. Next, a rabbit with stripes like a zebra! In just one small area of Southeast Asia, scientists have found half a dozen new species of large mammals—since 1992! "That's an incredible rate of discovery," said Gary. After all, since 1900 only about a dozen new species of large mammals have been discovered. Half of them had been found right near where we would be going.

The very things that might make our destination seem scary also made it the best place for us to look for a new bear.

Would you be too scared to go there? "Why go to a dangerous place when you could stay safe at home?" people asked us. We always answered the same way. Yes, it might be dangerous, but the chance to discover something new was just too exciting to pass up.

Still, we worried. All sorts of things could go wrong. What if the golden bear was gone when we got there? What if it turned out we had made a mistake, and the golden bear was nothing new? What if we were just plain wrong?

This little spirit house perched in a tree is scarcely bigger than a birdhouse.

"If you're too scared to be wrong, you're never going to do anything important," said Gary. "A good scientist has the duty to be wrong."

The *duty to be wrong?*

"Why, yes," the professor continued patiently. Scientists are always coming up with new ideas or theories, trying to test each one to see which is right—just like a detective trying to solve a mystery. Scientists call their theories *hypotheses.* "If you come up with lots of hypotheses, some of them are bound to be wrong," Gary said. "But if you don't have hypotheses, it's impossible to solve mysteries—at least that's what Sherlock Holmes says."

We'd have a lot to do before leaving on the eighteen hours of flights from Chicago to Cambodia that June. We'd need shots against tropical diseases like typhoid, hepatitis, and Japanese encephalitis. We'd need to get pills to protect us against malaria. We'd have to read up on Southeast Asia's wildlife, geography, and people. We'd need to contact other wildlife lovers in Southeast Asia who might have seen or heard of golden bears. And yes, we would need a bit of courage, too. This Gary had in ample supply. "Bandits might take our money," Gary resolved, "but they're not getting our bear hairs!"

in the market for bears

Sun Hean pulled his spotless white Camry over to the side of the dirt road at the city of Kampong Som. He'd arrived in Cambodia ahead of us, and had picked Gary and me up at the airport in the capital, Phnom Penh, just a few days before. Our expedition had officially begun.

Like all towns in Cambodia, Kampong Som had a lively market. Smiling men and women, often wearing bamboo hats to shield their faces from the sun, were selling everything you could imagine —and some stuff you might not want to.

Right on the street or in open-front stores, you can buy fresh, fragrant French bread, fly swatters, wedding dresses, Teletubbies key chains, chainsaws, watches.

We saw strange tropical fruits that looked like they grew on Mars: red, hairy rambutan, sweet and juicy. Eggplant-colored mangosteen, which smell like apples. Grapelike clusters of brown, papery-skinned lychee. Fat, luscious dragonfruit, which look like something in between a giant beet and a tropical fish.

But we also found even stranger items for sale. Swallows and rats roasted on skewers like shish kabobs. Live cobras, frogs, and turtles awaited the soup pot. The dried tails of elephants, the whiskers of tigers, and the gall bladders of bears were sold as medicine and good-luck charms. Water bugs and crickets sizzled in woks of hot oil. Folks here eat fried bugs for snacks like we might munch popcorn.

Yuk! We didn't want any of those! Besides, we had already eaten eggs, rice, and vegetables in a roadside restaurant. We always let Sun Hean order for us. But one night when he had gone to bed early, Gary and I learned what a mistake it was to order

food in a Cambodian restaurant without our host's help. Looking for a vegetarian dinner, I had ordered an item that translated to "Fragrant Flower Soup." I was served a bowl full of animal kidneys, intestines, livers, and a pancreas or two!

Sun Hean leaned out of the car window at Kampong Som to ask one of the shopkeepers: Did she know, by any chance, where we might find a moon bear?

She didn't ask what a young, well-dressed Cambodian, a middle-aged sunburned blonde, and a silver-haired professor from America might want with a bear. She was an animal dealer. She knew that people buy animals in Cambodia for many reasons. Sometimes for pets. Sometimes for dinner.

TOP: Fried bug snacks.
BOTTOM: A villager holds up the tall, spearlike horns of the newly discovered Saola, and the shorter horns of the goat-like serow.

Clouded leopards still prowl the forests of Southeast Asia.

Sometimes for medicine. Many of the animals she sells are illegal to buy or sell, so she didn't ask questions.

What we wanted with a bear, though, was so strange she couldn't have possibly guessed it. We wanted only to pull out, with my eyebrow tweezers, a few of its hairs—all in the name of science.

Wait a minute—what were we doing looking for a bear in a city market in the first place? Aren't the animals supposed to be in the jungle?

There are wonderful jungles in Southeast Asia, some of the oldest and richest in the world. In these steamy forests live clouded leopards, tigers, elephants, wild oxen with bluish coats, weasel-like civets, apes that sing, and deer with fangs—as well as at least two different species of bears. But what are the chances that any of them—especially one new to science—will run out of its hiding place, right in front of you, the moment you show up with your tweezers?

Just about zero. But the jungle isn't the only place to find new animals.

In fact, every one of the six new species of mammals other scientific teams have discovered in Southeast Asia had been found in villages, in private zoos, or in markets like this one. Scientists discovered the new 200-pound antelope, called the saola, by finding its horns for sale in villages in Vietnam. The zebra-striped rabbit was first noticed when a scientist saw its pelt for sale while shopping for groceries in Laos. And a yellow hog—described by science only once before, way back in 1892, and thought extinct—was rediscovered by a team of scientists in a villager's hut. They were served it for dinner!

This, of course, proves that species "new" to science aren't always new. Often, the local people know about them perfectly well. Which was why it was so important on our expedition that we talk with local people — like the shopkeeper at the market at Kampong Som.

Well, she said, she'd had a bear for sale earlier that day . . . but just that morning she'd sold it to someone from another city. What would happen to it there? we wondered. It might be someone's pet now — or someone's lunch. In many areas of Asia, particularly Japan and Korea but also here in Cambodia, people eat bears, especially the paws, use their organs for medicine, and hope to become strong like a bear.

The shopkeeper said she didn't know the bear's fate. But one thing she could tell us for sure: we'd have no trouble finding bears in this town. People captured them all the time.

In fact, by the time we checked out the market, we had already met the most important bear in town. Our first stop was the palm plantation where the golden bear Sun Hean had heard about lived.

She was smaller than we expected, and more beautiful, too. Her face was so pale, it reminded me of the faces of angels in paintings. Her mane, black on the sides and gold on the top, seemed to fit her like a shining halo. Except for her face and the dark at the mane and the edge of the ears, she was all different shades of gold. Some parts of her fur were as gold as

a rainforest orchid. Others were as gold as glistening honey. And some parts were nearly orange, like the robes monks wear at Buddhist temples.

But her gorgeous coat hung loosely on her body. At about two years of age, she should have weighed at least 200 pounds, but she looked like she weighed 125 at best. She was so thin we could see her ribs. We worried about her health. We wished we could set her free.

Carefully, slowly, we enticed her over to the side of her leafy outdoor cage. She seemed suspicious at first. But then, slowly padding on her leathery, pigeon-toed paws, she stepped toward us from the shadows. She opened her nostrils wide: mmmm! She could smell the marshmallows and the milk.

The golden bear particularly loved the sweet milk. She lapped eagerly with her long, thin, pink tongue. Sun Hean held the can for her. Gary

took notes on her appearance. I plucked hairs from her head with the tweezers and stuffed them into test tubes. Everything was going well.

Then Sun Hean, squatting close to the cage, withdrew the can to enlarge the opening for the hungry bear. But the "table service" wasn't fast enough. She grew impatient. Her head lunged out between the bars with astonishing speed and snapped at Sun Hean's knee with a snarl! But brave Sun Hean only made a joke. "If I get a scar," he said, "I can show my professor in America this is how the wildlife thinks about me!" Amazingly, her bite didn't even break the skin.

We spoke with the man who had captured her. He worked for the palm plantation owner. Sun Hean translated. He said she'd been caught as a cub less than a mile from here, more than a year before. He'd been out hunting for wild pigs when he saw this beautiful little golden cub. Where was her mother? we wondered. The man said he didn't know. But he thought his boss might like her as a present, so he brought her home. She used to have company in her cage, he told us—a black male bear who had been caught in the same area.

We'd heard about that bear earlier. We had hoped to pluck hair from him so his DNA could be compared with hers. But two months ago, the man told us, the black bear had died.

We were sad to hear that. The poor, thin golden bear must be lonely.

And it was bad news for our project, too. We needed the hairs of a black bear from the same area for comparison with the golden bear's DNA. If the DNA were very different, it would mean we had a brand-new species. If the DNA were similar, that would be a different story. We might have found a new color of a known species. Or, we might have discovered that young moon bears sometimes start out blond but then outgrow it, as some human children do.

We didn't know, but it was clear what we would have to do next: we would have to find another black bear, caught in this same area, to compare with our mystery golden bear.

Though lots of new fish, worms, and insects are discovered every year, large new mammals are rare. In the 1900s, there were only a few. The okapi, a short, striped forest giraffe with a long blue tongue; the giant forest hog; the mountain nyala, an antelope; and the bonobo, or pygmy chimpanzee, were discovered in Africa. The Chacoan peccary, a relative of the pig, was found in South America. The oxlike kouprey was discovered in Asia.

Then, just when everyone thought all the big mammals had been discovered, came 1992 and a new era of discovery. A whole slew of new animals was suddenly discovered in less than a decade—all in Southeast Asia! Let's meet some of them.

The saola: When a team of Vietnamese-American scientists found the first sets of horns of this animal in 1992 at a village market in Vietnam, they knew they were onto something important. The long, thin, tapered horns looked like those of no other animal in Asia. And when the animal itself was finally found alive—two whole years later— researchers were astonished: here was a beautiful, 200-pound antelope that scientists

Saola.

never knew existed. The saola is a striking animal, with fur the color of chestnuts offset by dramatic white stripes above the hooves and around the face. It lives in the steep, forested Annamite Mountains on the border between Laos, Cambodia, and Vietnam.

Four new or rediscovered muntjacs: Muntjacs are also known as barking deer because, when alarmed, they bark like dogs. Two different species of these primitive little deer with pointy fangs were already known in Southeast Asia in 1990—but that number soon tripled with the following discoveries.

The giant muntjac. Its existence was documented in

1899, when a photo of its antlers was published in a scientific journal—but no one paid any attention. Nearly a century later, teams of scientists from the Wildlife Conservation Society started seeing really big muntjac antlers in Laotian villages and shops in the Annamites. Then, in March 1994, while visiting a local general's private zoo, the scientists found the animal that went with the twenty-inch antlers. It was a new species, larger than the other species of muntjacs, with a short, broad tail, a gray-brown coat, a handsome black stripe on the forehead, and white on the belly.

Roosevelt's barking deer. In 1929, one of President Theodore Roosevelt's sons shot and killed a barking deer with a bright orange cap and tiny antlers less than an

Giant muntjac.

Annamite muntjac.

Putao muntjac.

inch long. Then nobody ever saw one again until the mid-1990s—when Wildlife Conservation Society researchers ran into hunters who had killed several. They had rediscovered a species everyone thought had vanished!

The Annamite muntjac. This species looks much like the Roosevelt's barking deer and was almost simultaneously discovered in Vietnam and in Laos by different teams of scientists working in the Annamite Mountains in the mid-1990s. By 1998, the two teams agreed they had discovered the same new species. With a crown of orange fur as long as the tiny antlers, the Annamite muntjac has blackish fur, dark legs, and a short tail with white edges.

The Putao muntjac. Standing only twenty inches tall at the shoulder and weighing only twenty-five pounds, this muntjac is one of the tiniest deer in the world. Wildlife Conservation Society researcher Alan Rabinowitz discovered it in 1999 when a hunter stepped out of a dense evergreen forest in northern Myanmar (formerly Burma) carrying one he had killed on his back.

Indochinese striped rabbit: How would you like to go to the grocery store and discover a new species? That's almost what happened to Wildlife Conservation Society researcher Rob Timmins in 1998. He first found the skins of this short-eared, zebra-striped rabbit at a food market in the foothills of the Annamite Mountains in Laos. Later, live animals were discovered in both Vietnam and Laos.

Yellow hog or Indochinese warty hog: Way back in 1892, a naturalist-priest based in Shanghai, China, received a gift from friends in Vietnam: two pig skulls that looked like no others he'd ever seen. But he never saw the pig itself, and the skulls got lost in a big museum in China. More than a century later, in 1995, a team of scientists led by George Schaller of the Wildlife Conservation Society sat down to dinner in an Annamite villager's hut in Laos. The scientists noticed that the skull of the pig they were eating looked different. It turned out to match the lost skulls from a century before! Still, no scientist has photographed or seen a live yellow hog. Maybe you'll be the one to do that someday!

TOP: Common muntjac. BOTTOM: White-handed gibbon.

the elephant mountains

"No problem," said Sun Hean. "Many people have bears in Cambodia!" So off we went, looking for more bears in town.

We stopped at a fancy hotel. Along paths lined with blooming flowers and tall bamboo, the hotel had a backyard zoo. In big, clean cages, swinging from tires and ropes, we found gibbons — apes with long arms and rich whooping voices, who sing duets with their mates at dawn. A golden cat slept in the shade. And there were four young bears wrestling and tumbling across their cage's cement floor — but they were the wrong kind of bear.

We knew Cambodia had only two known species of bear. One is named for the sun: the sun bear has a patch on the

chest that often is sunrise orange. The other is named for the moon: the moon bear wears a white V on its chest, like a crescent moon.

LEFT: Sun bear.
RIGHT: Moon bear.

The two bears are as different as day and night. The sun bear is small, about the size of a big dog, with sleek, black hair, tiny ears, and a wrinkly face, sort of like a rottweiler. Sun bears spend much of their time in trees, and prefer lowland rainforest. Moon bears are large, shaggy beasts, sometimes weighing 500 pounds. With their thick coat of black hair and their bushy manes, moon bears don't look like they belong in the tropics at all—but here they are. (Another mystery.) They have big round ears. They prefer mountain forests. Our golden bear definitely looked more like a moon bear than a sun bear. So we needed a moon bear for our DNA comparison.

Next we stopped at a fruit farm to talk with the workers there. Yes, they said, they could tell us where to find a bear. One of their friends snared a bear in the forest, just a few miles' walk from the farm! He's keeping

it in a cage at his mountain camp until he can sell it for a lot of money, they told us.

What kind of bear had he captured?

Finding out was unexpectedly difficult. Language was the problem. The Khmer word for bear, Sun Hean explained to us, is *kla khmum*, which means "honey-eating tiger." But just as in the United States (where a Coke might be called "pop" in one area and "soda" in another), in Cambodia people use different words in different areas for the same thing. In the province where Sun Hean grew up, people called the sun bear *kla khmum chruk*, or "honey-eating pig tiger." He said they called the moon bear *kla khmum chkai*—"honey-eating dog tiger." But the workers who grew up here, in a different province from Sun Hean, called this bear *kla khmum krabei*, or "honey-eating buffalo tiger."

What kind of bear was it? Was it a sun bear or moon bear? Or could it be a new species?

There was only one way to find out. We hired one of the men as a guide to take us to the camp in the Elephant Mountains the next day.

At dawn, rain hung over the mountains like the breath of a dragon. We could see it from the window of our little hotel. In Kampong Som, our rooms were much like those in an American hotel, except for a few details. We had air conditioning (thank goodness—we came into our rooms drenched with sweat every day) and hot and cold running

water. But you can't drink or even brush your teeth with tap water, or you'll get sick. Instead, there is a thermos of boiled water, often still warm, to drink. There are no shower curtains, so water sprays all over the bathroom—we had to move the towels and toilet paper out of the way. We were perfectly comfortable, but we were eager to get into the wilderness.

We were excited about our hike. We'd have to be careful, Sun Hean warned us: there are cobras in the forest, as well as leopards and tigers. Wild elephants live here, giving the mountains their name. We might see signs of wild bears today, too, we hoped: claw marks on trees, holes clawed in the dirt to dig up ground-dwelling bees, and the resting platforms bears sometimes make in trees from springy broken branches.

We began our hike along a track as wide as a bulldozer. In fact, a bulldozer had been here, to make a road for loggers. But after an hour's walk, the jungle began to reappear. Crickets sang around us. Vines seemed to scramble along the ground. Young saplings shielded us from the daily monsoon rain. We listened to the tink and whistle of strange birds and the whir and buzz of cicadas.

After an hour of walking, we crossed a knee-deep stream. "Many leeches, maybe," Sun Hean warned us. You usually can't tell when a leech has bitten you. Leech drool contains a natural painkiller, like novocaine —but still, Sun Hean didn't like finding the sluglike parasites in his socks, full of his blood. (Neither do I. But it's not as bad as finding one in your underwear!)

We'd hiked for only a couple of hours when we found the little camp. It was just a tin roof held up by pillars, sheltering two tiny cages. In one cage huddled a terrified muntjac, a little deer standing only two feet tall. Another cage was raised above the ground on blocks of wood. The wire cage was only inches bigger than the bear cub inside—a black bear with big, rounded ears and a white V on the chest. "Oh, *yes!*" cried Sun Hean.

We had found our comparison bear. The "honey-eating buffalo tiger" was a moon bear after all.

The man who had captured her appeared to greet us. He was a poor man, maybe thirty or forty years old, with tattered clothes. Trying to be gracious to his foreign guests, he opened the door to her cage to give us a better view of his bear. We could see she was terrified of him. Her ears slammed back against her head. She stepped forward gingerly, as if her feet hurt. The man waved a stick at her, and she rushed back into the horrid little cage.

We all wished desperately we could rescue her. Why couldn't we just buy her? We would have happily stayed in a cheaper hotel, or skipped a few meals, to get her out of there. But if we bought her, what next? Sun

Hean told us the national zoo outside Phnom Penh was full of rescued bears. They couldn't hold any more.

Could we just let her go? We'd thought about that with the golden bear, too. That wouldn't work—a baby bear can't survive alone in the forest any more than a human baby could. Even older bears turned loose in new territories are often doomed. Most of the good land is already "owned" by other bears—and they don't usually appreciate newcomers. By their second spring of life, female bears share their mother's territory, and the mother bear chases other bears away. Young male bears have a harder time. They have to strike out and find new land of their own. To find a home, young males may have to travel hundreds of miles and face many dangers: other males, roads, dangerous terrain, hunters' guns, and snares. You can see why, once a male bear finally finds his own territory, he defends it bravely from other bears.

Could we take the cub home? That wouldn't work, either: laws meant to protect endangered animals like moon bears make it illegal to take wild animals out of the country except under very special circumstances.

And there was another problem as well: if we bought this bear, we would be rewarding this man for capturing her. Then he would go out and hunt another one. Two bears would be gone from the wild instead of one—and the man who had kidnapped them would look for a third, and a fourth . . .

We couldn't rescue the little cub any more than we could set the golden bear free. But we could do something else. Sun Hean, as deputy director of Cambodia's Wildlife Protection Office, was working to strengthen and enforce his country's laws to protect animals like these. And our scientific project could help. Discovering a beautiful new bear could help the people of Cambodia appreciate just how special their wildlife is and inspire them to respect and protect it.

Sadly, we left the little bear behind. We took away only her hairs for science. Her future was uncertain. But she would be part of a discovery that would honor bears forever—a discovery whose importance would outlive all of us.

We continued to walk into the forest, hoping to see signs of wild bears. "Quick, quick please!" Gary and I heard Sun Hean call ahead of us. "Very large, very big!"

We hurried toward him, excited. Had he found a wild bear? A tiger? A leopard? A giant wild ox?

No—our wildlife encounter lay on the mud beside Sun Hean's boot. At first it looked to be a creature the size of a man's thumb, but it quickly stretched out toward Gary's foot. It was as long as a banana—the most monstrous leech we had ever seen!

The rain began to pour as we slogged on through the mud. The leech probably liked it. The wild bears, leopards, muntjacs, and monkeys all stayed snug in their hides and holes. Their footprints dissolved in the rain. The next day, Sun Hean promised us, we would take a ferry to Koh Kong and venture into an even wilder area. Maybe we would see signs of bear there. But now, he advised, we should turn back.

Our guide, the man we'd met at the fruit orchard, would be glad to get us home safely. But he was nervous. Earlier, on our walk, he had confided to Sun Hean that he'd seen strangers in the distance after we'd left the camp. Strangers—so what, we thought? But the last time he had guided people in this forest, just a few months before, he had met some strangers he wished he'd never encountered. They were bandits—and they had kidnapped the whole party! The group was held prisoner for days in a jungle hut and beaten with sticks until their families paid ransom for their release. Gary, Sun Hean, and I wished he had told us about that *before* taking us into the Elephant Mountains.

He never saw the strangers again. What a relief! But on the way back, we heard an explosion from the direction from which we had just come. Thunder? I asked. No, answered our Cambodian friend. He knew the sound well. He answered matter-of-factly: "Land mine."

club med
for bears

Standing on his hind legs, Stripe, a 250-pound moon bear with yellowish eyes, was looking Gary right in the face. Luckily, they were separated by the partially closed window of our Jeep! Gary and I were safe inside the car, and around us stretched a sea of bears.

We weren't in the forest. We had left Cambodia. Now Gary and I were in Thailand, not far from a big town. But we had never seen so many bears in one place at one time.

As Stripe investigated Gary, I noticed another bear was chewing on one of our back tires. He soon switched to trying to pry off the hubcap with his claws. We decided to pull away — slowly — before he took it away as a toy.

We could see another five bears within

twenty feet of us, and another ten bears beyond. Some soaked in shallow pools. Sitting upright just like people, with their arms spread out, they looked like fat old men in the whirlpool bath at a health club. While we sweated in the Jeep, other bears relaxed on the grass beneath cool shade trees. Some just stood there watching us as if we were a TV program. Still others lunched on cooked rice mixed with dog biscuits. Their meals were delivered twice a day, steaming hot, by workers on the green food truck we were following in our Jeep. All the bears seemed happy and relaxed. It seemed we were in a tropical Club Med for bears!

But this was no resort. It wasn't a zoo, either. Banglamung Wildlife Breeding Center was like no place we had ever been before. For Gary and me, it was a great place to look for more golden bears.

We had said goodbye to Sun Hean the night before. He had been a wonderful host in Cambodia. After we had left the Elephant Mountains, as he'd promised, the three of us traveled north to the Cardamom Mountains. To keep us safe from bandits, Sun Hean had organ-

ized a team of forest patrolmen with machine guns to accompany us as we explored the jungle. We all rode on motorcycles for ten hours along the bumpy, slippery logging roads that had only recently been cut into the jungle.

It was a wild, exciting ride. It was fun watching the jungle whiz by in a green blur. It was even better when we stopped to admire the amazing forest around us. And we stopped a lot—usually because one of us fell off the motorcycle into the mud! Imagine a forest where grasses tower 100 feet tall. (Bamboo can grow as tall as trees, but it is really a kind of grass.) Thorny rattan vines turned, twisted, and climbed over the ground. Orchids bloomed in the treetops.

"These forests are bound to be loaded with moon bears!" Gary predicted as we surveyed the jungle. But we saw no bears that day. Nobody we met along the way had ever heard of a golden bear.

Still, we weren't ready to go home. Even before we left the United States for Cambodia, Gary and I had heard of two other places, both in Thailand, where we could look for more golden bears. So this was where we went next.

Now, at Banglamung Wildlife Breeding Center, we were just outside the Thai seaside city of Pattaya. You usually wouldn't think of a shore resort as a good place to look for bears—but by now we had begun to expect surprises everywhere.

"I've never seen so many moon bears in my life!" Gary exclaimed from the Jeep. Most of them were adults, and some weighed more than 400 pounds. "These are very big, impressive animals," Gary remarked, "just wonderful!"

Some 60 moon bears lived at Banglamung—as well as about 15 sun bears, 50 macaque monkeys, 4 furry-tailed

The bearlike binturong is actually a kind of civet.

civets called binturongs, and about 200 dogs.

The place wasn't originally set up for them at all. Banglamung had opened two decades before as part of a network of centers the Thai Royal Forest Department created to breed endangered native pheasants and deer. During the 1970s and '80s, hunters had wiped out many of Thailand's wonderful species of birds and mammals. The Thai Royal Forest Department wanted to breed and release pheasants and deer so the forests wouldn't be empty anymore.

Finally, in 1992, Thailand made it illegal to kill, capture, or sell native animals. To enforce the new law, when Royal Forest Department officers found bears, monkeys, or other wild animals illegally held captive, they would take them away. But where to put them?

Around the Pattaya area, the officers took them to Banglamung. Once fourteen bears came in on one day—all from a single restaurant. They were rescued just in time! So Banglamung's "breeding center" became a sort of refugee center, too—a halfway house for animals who were born wild, taken captive, and finally rescued.

A private charity stepped in to help. The Thai Society for the Conservation of Wild Animals raised money to build big, grassy outdoor pens for the moon and sun bears of Banglamung. They built spacious, tree-filled cages for the binturongs and monkeys. Volunteers came from all over the world to help care for the animals. Soon, they found themselves taking care of about 200 unwanted dogs, too.

As dogs barked, pheasants shrieked, and gibbons sang,

Gary and I surveyed the bears around us. We saw bears with bushy manes, bears with stumpy legs, bears with long black fur. We saw shy bears and quarrelsome bears: when bears argue, they stand on their hind feet. Hunching over slightly, they make hideous wrinkled faces at one another, showing their huge yellow teeth and snarling, but usually they don't hurt each other. We saw muddy bears, dusty bears, wet bears. We saw pudgy bears, fat bears, and some really, *really* fat bears—one was named Lardy!

But we saw no golden bears.

Incredibly, though, we saw *different* bears that no scientist had recorded before!

As we toured Banglamung's 180-acre compound, we found several mainly dark moon bears with beautiful light markings. Stripe was almost like a panda. He had a handsome, pale face with dark brown fur circling his eyes, all framed by his dark mane. Two other bears, named Romeo

and Louis, had light faces. Gary took careful notes on their appearance. "The rear claws on that bear seem to have an ivory tinge," he would say into the tape recorder. Or, "this bear's forehead seems slightly less sloping than the others." When you're solving mysteries, sometimes you never know what turns out to be important—so you have to pay attention to everything.

Did the pale-faced, pandalike bears all come from the same area? we wondered. Did they come, perhaps, from the same area as our golden bear? If so, they might be another variant of our golden bear. Or maybe they were a new species themselves! Or perhaps they were an unknown color of the normally black moon bear.

Their DNA held the answer. But first we would need to find out where these bears came from.

We spoke with the director of the Thai Society for the Conservation of Wild Animals, Gary van Zuylen. He was an Australian who had chosen to make Thailand his home. But alas, he told us, no one knew where most of Banglamung's bears had originally lived. By the time most of them had been rescued by forest officers, they were usually very, very far from home.

Romeo was an exception. He had come from the Thai side of the Thai-Cambodia border, just north of the Cardamom ranges where we had traveled on our motorcycles with Sun Hean—and still part of the mountain range where the golden bear had lived. A forest officer said that Thai police had heard the crack of gunfire—probably Romeo's mother being killed—and followed the sound to arrest the poacher and take Romeo away.

Romeo wasn't with the other bears in the outdoor enclosure. He shared a spacious cage with a black female bear. Both were friendly and calm. They let us scratch the backs of their large round ears. They let us touch their wet noses through the bars of their cage. Taking samples of Romeo's hair was easy.

Now we had hair from *two* different kinds of mystery bears, and our scientific quest was now *twice* as exciting as before! But we still had one more destination to visit: a zoo run by soldiers in the Thai town of Lop Buri, 125 miles north of Pattaya, where we had heard there might be another golden bear.

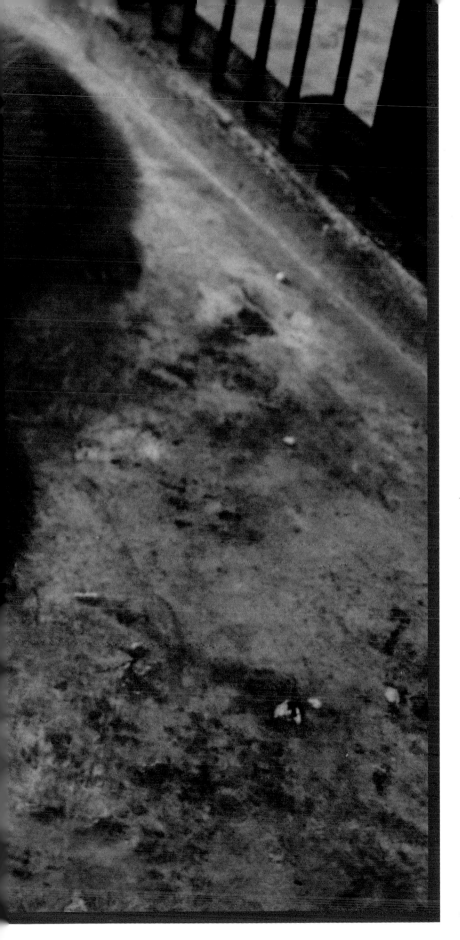

a lion among bears

The first thing you see as you near the bear enclosure at Lop Buri Zoo is a billboard. "Mary's Bear Home," the big sign tells you, was a gift to the zoo from Mary Hutton, an Australian with her own organization called Free the Bears Fund. All the bears who live here, we read, were born wild, then captured, and finally rescued from the illegal wildlife trade. Now, thanks to Mary and her Free the Bears Fund, they're safe in spacious indoor cages and enjoy a big outdoor yard with two bathing pools and plenty of trees to climb.

As Gary and I approached the cages, we heard a strange sound—sort of a cross between the hum of a sump pump and the nickering of a goat. It was coming from one of the two sun bears!

I had heard the sound before. Back in New Hampshire, a friend of mine, Ben Kilham, raises orphaned baby American black bears. Bear cubs normally make this sound when they suck milk from their mothers. Ben's babies made this sound when they nursed from a bottle—and they also made it when they sucked on Ben's ears.

The sun bear in Mary's Bear Home was nearly adult. But he was making the nickering sound. He was sucking on his own paw—just like a frightened child who sucks his thumb. The sun bear must have still missed his mother.

Next we noticed another sad thing. One of the moon bears had only three feet. His name was Stumpy. He had been rescued from a poacher who was caught in the act of cutting off one of his paws to make bear paw soup.

Then I saw something *really* alarming. A lion was living in the bear enclosure!

"Gary, look!" I cried. A tawny, fat male lion with a big fluffy mane was in among the bears! What was he doing there? And strangely, he seemed to be chewing a piece of bok choy—a sort of Asian celery. It seemed odd that a lion should like celery that much.

Then Gary and I realized what was wrong. The "lion's" mane surrounded the face of a bear.

"This is the largest, blondest bear we've ever seen!" Gary exclaimed.

The author videotapes Dave, a bear unlike any other before recorded.

We had just met Bertha. Big and shaggy, she was clearly an adult bear—proof that the gold color wasn't just something that certain young bears have but then outgrow. And, nearly as exciting, another large moon bear in the big cage looked like Stripe. This big, pale-faced, eye-ringed male was named Dave. His mane was longer than Stripe's and the back half of his body was much lighter.

At Lop Buri, we had hit a bear jackpot! And you can guess what we had to do next: find out where these bears came from and pull some of their hairs.

But we faced a new problem. We had learned a few phrases of the beautiful Thai language—like Sa-wa-di for greeting people, mai pen rai ("what will be, will be"—a useful reply when told your plans have gone wrong), and, of course, the words for sun bear (mee maa), moon bear (mee kwai), and the color gold (thong, pronounced "tahng"). But we didn't know enough Thai to explain what we wanted and why. How would we find out where the bears had come from? And what would the zookeepers say if they found two foreign strangers pulling out hair from their bears without permission?

Sun bears love to play and climb.

Sangphet Unkeaw came to our rescue. First, the young zookeeper mercifully let us call him something we could pronounce—Tom. Second, because he could speak English, he agreed to translate for us so we could talk to the zoo director and find out where the bears came from. And third, he knew a way to make plucking out bear hair safe and easy.

The bears' indoor cage was equipped with what's known in the zoo trade as a "squeeze cage." The bears don't really get squeezed. A portion of the cage is fitted with three walls that can move and confine the animal to a small space. It's designed so veterinarians can give animals shots and other treatments without having to tranquilize them. The bears are usually happy to go into the squeeze cage, Tom told us. They know they'll get a tasty banana as a reward.

So into the squeeze cage went Bertha—and into our test tube went her hair. Dave was next. And as long as we were at it, we got hairs from

the four black moon bears, too. "Why not?" asked Gary. We really didn't need them, but then again, who knew? They might come in handy.

Next we visited the zoo director. Dapper and cheerful, Colonel Wirat Phupiangjai had scoured the zoo records for us. With Tom translating, he told us he had good news: though no one knew where the black moon bears had originally lived, he had found the story of Bertha and Dave. They both came from the same place.

Both had been captured as cubs on the slopes of a bamboo forest in the Louang Prabang Mountains, on the Thai side of the border with northern Laos. The same family of farmers had caught both of them at separate times; they wanted them as pets because of their unusual color. The colonel showed us the little town where they had lived on a map. Gary had already plotted the locations of the other golden and pale-faced bears we had found. Adding this one, he saw that all the points strung out in an arc that ran right through northern Laos.

We would return with our bear hairs to the United States in a few days, but it would be weeks before the DNA would be analyzed. We didn't know what we would find. But already we were thinking about a new expedition—to Laos!

In Asia, people have loved bears for centuries. Because they're so smart, they star in circus acts, dance in street shows, and live in people's houses. People have taught performing bears to roller skate, ride bicycles, and walk on stilts. In Russia, in the nineteenth century, there was even a sort of bear college, the Academy for Training Young Bears. In Turkey, India, and Greece, bears still dance alongside performers, although humane agencies are trying to stop the practice. And despite laws against keeping bears as pets, in China many people do so anyway. The bears even sometimes help with household chores: they carry laundry on their backs alongside their owners as they travel from the river back to the house.

But in many parts of Asia, people love bears in a different way: they love to eat them.

Bear parts are eaten as delicacies and sold as medicine. In Asia, many people believe eating bears can make people strong. Bear paws are eaten to make the hands strong like a bear's. Bear blood is believed to cure nervousness. The bones are thought to cure joint disease. People even eat bear fat to try to cure baldness!

But the part of the bear most prized is a little fig-shaped organ,

an accessory to digestion: the gall bladder. Bear gall is one of the most popular and expensive medicines in Asia. The Chinese have prized it for 3,000 years, believing it a sort of cure-all. They use it to treat almost everything from diabetes to liver cancer, from heart disease to tooth decay.

For many centuries, bear parts were used sparingly in Asian medicine. "At one time," Judy Mills and Christopher Servheen, two experts on the trade in bear parts, wrote in a recent report for the World Wildlife Fund, "there were so many bears and so few people that using bears as medicine, food and pets probably did little harm."

But all that's changed. China's human population is now more than 1 billion. More and more people in Hong Kong, Japan, Singapore, and Taiwan want bear gall as a cure-all. Some rich people in Asia take bear gall as often as they can. The ex-president of the Hyundai Corporation, Jung Ju Young, publicly brags that he

takes bear gall as you or I might take a daily vitamin.

Boasts like that drive the price of bear gall higher and higher. Because rich people like Jung Ju Young are willing to pay for it, bear gall can now sell for eighteen times its weight in gold! And that "has put a price on the head of every bear," the World Wildlife Fund report said, "making them all worth more dead than alive."

Does bear gall actually work? This is the really sad part. Unlike most other animal body parts used in Asian medicine, bear gall really does contain an ingredient that can ease some health problems, like gallstones. It's called ursodeoxycholic acid (UCDA, for short). UCDA can be made easily and cheaply in the laboratory for about sixteen cents per pill. But people like the rich Hyundai executive would rather buy real bear gall. They think paying all that money for a luxury makes them look important. They say real bear gall works better.

Scientists agree this is wrong. And they agree on something else as well: as a result of the greed for bear-based medicines, Asia is running out of moon and sun bears. Some conservationists fear that grizzlies, black bears, and polar bears will be next.

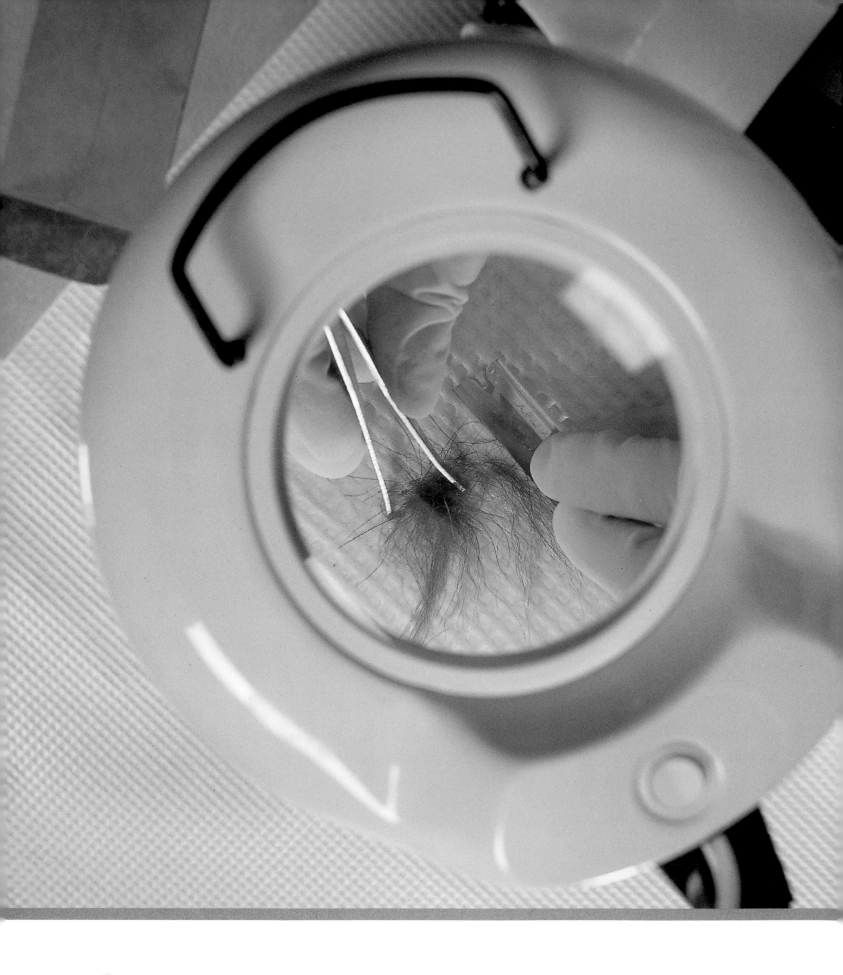

Bear hairs under the magnifying lens are scrutinized for the best bulbs—the parts with living cells and the best DNA.

cracking the code

Back home in the States, while Gary and I rested up from our trip, our bear hairs embarked on a new journey of their own.

In a big padded box, our test tubes and their hairy cargo jetted from Gary's home in Chicago to Moscow, Idaho. Passing beneath the glass eyes of two mounted elk heads guarding the foyer of the University of Idaho's College of Natural Resources, the box was carried through a door, down a corridor, through more doors, and into a reception area. Finally it came to rest on a desk in a small corner room decorated with photos and cartoons of bears and kids' drawings and paintings.

Our samples had arrived at the office of Dr. Lisette Waits. But their real journey had just begun.

At Lisette's laboratory, the hairs we collected would be sliced, washed, and purified. In big, humming machines, the cells of the hair bulb would be spun, heated, and magnified. At different points in the process they would glow in the dark and get jolted with electricity. They would be changed into colorless liquid, turned into blue Jell-O, and be converted to glowing points of light. Only with the help of Lisette's sophisticated machines and powerful computers would the hairs we had plucked from live bears with eyebrow tweezers give up their secrets.

Lisette, a marathon runner and mother of two young boys, is a molecular geneticist who specializes in bears. From the time she was a little girl, she always wanted to solve mysteries about animals. At first she thought she'd be a marine biologist, studying the behavior of whales and walruses and seals. But everything changed in college when she took a course in genetics, the study of DNA. "I thought, Whoa!" she said, her brown eyes still wide with the surprise. "This seems like we can get such specific and definitive answers to questions that in field research would take years and years!"

Studying DNA, Lisette realized, could give her an almost magic short-cut to solving mysteries. For instance, she'd have to watch pods of dolphins for many years before she could figure out who was related to whom and how. By looking at DNA, she could tell within hours. Whoa!

When Lisette started college, scientists were already making breathtaking discoveries using molecular genetics. In the 1980s, two researchers announced that by tracing changes in DNA in blood samples taken from people around the world, they found that all people alive today are descendants of one woman who lived in Africa 200,000 years ago! And just a few years after that, DNA analysis was used to solve the riddle of the panda. DNA studies now prove the panda is not a relative of the raccoon, as some scientists thought, but instead is the earliest of the known species of living bears.

When Lisette was a graduate student, she had a chance to try these new molecular genetics techniques out on grizzly bears. She was invited to Yellowstone to visit. There she saw her first grizzly: a mother bear, and then her cub, came lumbering and playing over a hill. "It gave me goosebumps," she said. Everything about these bears enchanted her. "Even their

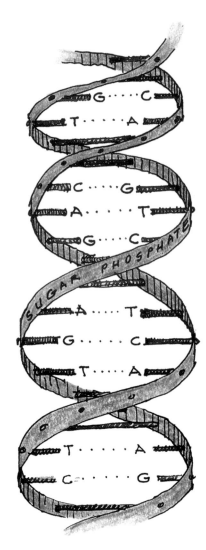

On the DNA molecule, the four different bases are arranged like the rungs on a spiral ladder.

DNA goes to the laundry: Dr. Lisette Waits washes contaminants from the DNA sample in a centrifuge.

gait," she said, "even the way they move. It's very beautiful. No other animal moves the way they do through the landscape." She fell in love with their power and wildness. And then she knew what she wanted to do for the rest of her life.

Lisette's parents were worried. Why don't you become a doctor instead? they asked. How in the world could anyone get a job combining molecular genetics and bear conservation?

But Lisette's advisor at school told her, "Do what you love. Be very, very good at it. And everything will be OK."

He was right. Lisette loves her job, combining two of her favorite things: bears and molecular genetics. In fact, Lisette runs the biggest lab for bear DNA in the world.

In her laboratory here, she's analyzing DNA from bears all over the world. With the help of students and assistants, Lisette is investigating how many grizzly and black bears share salmon around streams. She's discovering how often brown bears travel to mate with other brown bears at different oases in the Gobi Desert. She's counting how many black bears inhabit a certain study area in Minnesota and learning how they are related to each other.

DNA can tell you all these things, and more. You can even use it to travel back in time. But first, as Lisette explained, you have to crack the code.

Lisette uses a multichannel pipette to squirt the DNA samples into another set of tiny test tubes for the next reaction.

The secret recipe for all life is written in just four letters: *A, C, G,* and *T.* Each of these letters stands for a chemical called a nucleotide: *A* for adenine, *C* for cytosine, *G* for guanine, and *T* for thymine. Like a single letter of the alphabet, each nucleotide means nothing all by itself. But like letters strung together in a word, the order in which they appear in the

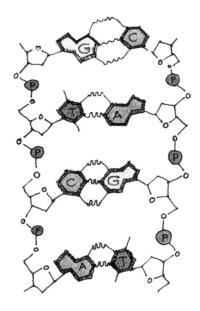

Adenine always pairs with thymine, and guanine with cytosine. The order in which they appear is what's important: each sequence is a set of instructions for how to make amino acids, the building blocks of life.

DNA molecule is what matters. The sequence of nucleotides in DNA gives the unique instructions for how to make each one of us—whether a bear, a scientist, a parrot, or a pine tree.

All of us—animals, plants, and people, too—share similarities in our DNA. Your DNA code is most similar to those of other people in your family. The instructions for making you are more like your parents' DNA than the DNA of your best friend. And her DNA is more like that of her grandmother's than her teacher's. Any person's DNA is more like a chimp's than an elephant's, and an elephant's DNA is more like a horse's than DNA from a fish. A fish's DNA is more like a frog's than a daisy's.

When you think about it, it makes perfect sense. Biology teaches us that all living creatures—from plants to people—came from a common ancestor more than 4 billion years ago. We're all different from one another because over time, DNA steadily changes, or mutates. (Sort of like your bike: as time goes by, it gets a ding here, a scrape there, and maybe you add a new bell or a basket or perhaps even a new seat.) Most mutations don't matter; some are bad, but a few are good. The good ones—happy accidents—stick around in the genetic code. They are passed down from generation to generation, because they help you adapt to the particular place you live, and let you leave more copies of the good mutation in the form of more children.

So the longer two people—or two species—have been separated from their common ancestor, the more mutations will have piled up. This is particularly true for a type of DNA that is found in special parts of the cell, called the mitochondria. Here, the intervals between mutations are almost like the tick-tocking of a clock, counting time. And that's one way Lisette uses the DNA code. By comparing the mutations of different DNA samples, she can tell how long ago different individuals, families, or species shared a common ancestor. In a sense, DNA is a time machine!

And that's not the only trick you can do with DNA. Like a magician, Lisette can even count the animals living in a given area without ever seeing them! All she has to do is have someone string up some low barbed wire around an irresistible bait. The bears slink under the wire to get the treat, leaving some hair behind. She can tell from differences in the DNA how many different individuals came.

"Sometimes the work is really challenging," Lisette told us, "but it's always exciting, too." And one of the best parts is that all this work in the laboratory can really help bears survive in the wild—by telling us things we might never be able to discover otherwise.

Lisette's lab is a series of rooms, occupying parts of two floors, filled with millions of dollars' worth of computers, centrifuges, heating and cooling devices, and all sorts of other whirring, humming machines. Some of the machines sport names that sound like comic book superheroes ("The Sequencer"). Others have nicknames (the lab's three polymerase chain reaction machines, which copy DNA, are nicknamed Bonnie, Clyde, and Wattana). Assistants in white lab coats and protective goggles are squirting chemicals into test tubes and mixing up gels that glow under fluorescent light. With the help of all these machines and chemicals, plus a computer, eventually Lisette will be able to read the sequence of nucleotides on the DNA.

Lisette's work is so different from what Gary, Sun Hean, and I had been doing that it seems impossible to believe that both are aspects of the same science! Yet we all knew that none of us could get our answer without the others.

It takes time to run these analyses, Lisette explained. There were lots of other samples ahead of us in line. And, she warned us, not every hair sample works out. Sometimes the bulb of the sample doesn't have live cells. Sometimes mold attacks the DNA in the samples. We had visited Southeast Asia during the wet season, when everything is moist; even your leather belt can grow mold in your suitcase. What if our hairs contained no DNA at all?

For months, we waited and wondered.

Like spies communicating in code, scientists use a special set of words when talking about the secret recipe for life that's written in each of our cells. Here's some of their vocabulary.

Nucleotide: The individual chemical elements of DNA — adenine, cytosine, guanine, and thymine. Like letters forming a word, every three nucleotides spell out the instructions for one amino acid.

Amino acids: Chemical compounds that link into chains to form the different proteins that make up all living cells. There are twenty different kinds of amino acids.

DNA: Short for deoxyribonucleic acid, DNA is the molecule containing the recipe for making everything that has ever lived. It's the stuff that determines whether you'll have green eyes or brown, black hair or blonde; it's

the reason you look like your parents and not like the mailman or the bus driver. DNA is way too small to see without special computers, but if you could blow it up it would look like a twisty, spiraling ladder. The rungs of the ladder are the important parts. Each rung is made of two nucleotides, because the bases always pair together: adenine always pairs with thymine, and guanine with cytosine.

Gene: The set of nucleotides that codes for one of the chains of amino acids, which form proteins. DNA is all these genes combined, all in a single molecule!

Mitochondria: All cells have different parts to them, just like a person's body has different organs. The mitochondria (mite-oh-CON-dree-uh) are the parts of the cell that produce the cell's energy. Mitochondria consume the oxygen we breathe and help us burn the food we eat. There are lots of mitochondria in each cell. DNA is found only in the mitochondria and one other part: the nucleus, a big, distinct blob full of DNA that's as easy to see under a microscope as the yellow in a fried egg. Though all DNA mutates, mutations in the nuclear DNA can often be reversed. That's one reason many scientists would rather look at the mitochondrial DNA, because the mitochondria can't repair mutations. It's easier to count the mutations that way.

The bear shown immediately above was found in China in 1988 by Dr. Gary Galbreath. It was the first golden moon bear discovered.

Finally, that October, Lisette sent Gary the results. Gary phoned Sun Hean and me, and he invited us to meet him in Chicago. What he had to say was so important that he wanted to tell us in person.

We met at a Chinese restaurant. Though Sun Hean and I were hungry, we hardly glanced at the menu. We were hungrier for Gary's news.

"The results are very exciting," Gary told us. "But they are exciting in a way I didn't expect!"

He paused. Sun Hean and I held our breath.

"Almost all the samples gave good results," he told us. That was a relief—but what did they say?

The professor continued, "All the golden

bears and all the pandalike bears were identical on all the nucleotides examined," he told us.

"Do we have a new species, then?" Sun Hean asked anxiously.

It certainly looked like it. Except for one thing: one of the black moon bears' DNA also matched those of the light bears!

"The genes are the same," said Gary. "So this suggests to me strongly that we're looking at two color phases of the same sort of bear."

We had discovered a new bear—just not a whole new species of bear. "Like the white tiger," I suggested—which is a rare light form or color phase of the Royal Bengal tiger. Imagine being the first person to discover a white tiger!

"Or the black leopard," added Sun Hean. Sometimes called black panthers, these inky-dark cats are actually the same species as the spotted leopard, even though they look very different.

"Yes," Gary agreed. Our golden bears were not a new species—but neither were they some weird genetic accident like a five-legged cow. "We've discovered something that's new," Gary told us. "That no one has documented this before is amazing."

We all paused to let the news sink in. Of course we were disappointed that the golden moon bear wasn't a whole new species. If it were, we would have discovered the first new species of bear in a century, the first new bear

Black leopard.

since the panda. And Gary, as senior scientist, would have had the honor of giving it a scientific name. Its first name would have had to be *Ursus* of course; but Gary had already picked out its second name: he wanted to name it *donruthi*, to honor his parents, Don and Ruth. Now *donruthi* would have to wait for another animal.

Still, the discovery of a brand-new color phase of the moon bear was important. But this wasn't what had gotten Gary so excited. The professor explained that the real news had come from the black moon bears whose hairs we had plucked almost by chance at Lop Buri—bears we hadn't expected to learn anything new from at all.

These bears' DNA proved so different from one another that Lisette had calculated their ancestors must have been evolving separately from one another for hundreds of thousands of years. Quite unexpectedly, we had stumbled onto a way to solve a mystery even more interesting than the identity of the golden bears. With their thick coats and fluffy manes, moon bears don't look like they belong in the hot, humid jungles of Southeast Asia. "How and when and where did these bizarre shaggy things get to be in this strange tropical place?" Gary had always wondered. "They are as out of place as an Eskimo in the tropics."

Now we had a way to find out. Like Lisette, we had found a way to use the DNA code as a time machine.

Changes in DNA record ancient histories. Remember, the more time passes, the more DNA changes. Because of the tick-tock of mutations, we could figure out which bears' DNA instructions were closest to the "original" and which were more recent.

We needed more samples—lots of them!—and we needed to know where each came from. But if we could do that, we could see how our bears sorted into lineages, or groups with closely related ancestors. We could plot the lineages on a map. We could map the oldest lineages and the younger ones and the very newest ones. And that would show us, roughly, the route the first moon bears took as they came south many hundreds of thousands of years ago and colonized the strange, tropical world of Southeast Asia.

"It's incredible!" said Gary. "After yanking hairs out of the moon bears we've met, we can find out where these big shaggy bears actually bumbled around a hundred thousand years ago. It's even more incredible than looking at fossils!"

But there was more. Once we had discovered all the bear lineages and matched them with a location, with our mitochondrial map in hand, a handful of hair from any bear could tell us where it came from. Maybe not as exact as a street address, but at least a general area.

So now we could find out where the many mystery bears at Lop Buri and Banglamung had originally lived in the wild. And if we knew where they came from, we could put them back! After all, we had learned that many of Thailand's forests were now empty. Because there were so few other bears already in residence, they wouldn't chase the rescued bears away. And because we'd be returning bears to where they came from, and not just randomly dumping them any-old-where in Thailand, they'd have the best chance at survival. Even their genes were made for this place.

We could never have guessed that Gary's whim to pluck the black bears of Lop Buri would bring us such a scientific bonanza! And neither could we have known, when we left the poor, caged cub behind in the Elephant Mountains camp, that she might help us free so many of her fellow moon bears in neighboring Thailand.

"This project has had more plot twists than one of your whodunits!" I said to Gary.

"That's why I love science," he replied.

Gary proposed a toast: "To the golden moon bear!" he said. We all clinked our glasses—and began to plan our next expedition.

TOP: Old meets new in modern Thailand.
BOTTOM: For our research we met and spoke with people from different hill tribes in northern Thailand, like this Akha lady. Her beautiful headdress is adorned with cowrie shells.

W e've made many expeditions to Southeast Asia since that dinner in October 1999. We visited the Annamite Mountains, where new species of antelope, hog, and rabbit were found. We interviewed hill tribes in Thailand and Laos about bears, and stayed in a house built on stilts in a Black Lahu village. We traveled again to Cambodia and marveled at the temple ruins of its ancient capital. We plucked many more bear hairs. We encountered many more surprises.

We met some wonderful people on our journeys. In the Annamite Mountains of Laos, we met people from different tribes and cultures. All of them helped us by telling us about bears. Along the way, we learned a lot about both people and animals.

At one village, we met people of the Liha tribe. They used to hunt by following groups of Asiatic wild dogs, or dholes, to their kill. The people would thank the dholes, take part of the meat, and leave the rest for the dogs. They never took more than they needed. But things are changing, the tribal elders told us. Foreigners have started to come to their mountains. They come to make fast money. They cut down the trees and capture the animals. And now the Liha don't see dholes anymore. They don't see bears or wild deer either. "Now," one old man told us sadly, "we don't know where they live."

At another village in Laos, we met a man who was sort of a village doctor. He was very old and wise. His name was Mo Vang, and he showed us a special treasure. It was a book—the only book in the whole village written in his tribe's native language. It was read at funeral services, reminding everyone that the dead are not forgotten, and that our ancestors are always important to us. But Mo Vang was sad. Only he and one other person, another old man, could read the book. Everyone else had forgotten, and the young people didn't want to learn. When Mo Vang and his elderly friend are gone, who will read the book? The world is changing quickly, he told us. The same changes that can hurt dholes, bears, and forests can threaten people, too. We need to hang on to what is important, Mo Vang told us, or it will be lost forever.

TOP: Buddhist nun with shaved head at one of Angkor's ancient temples. BOTTOM: Mo Vang holds the last book of his tribe.

Near Banglamung, back in Thailand again, we visited a Buddhist monk who had lived in a temple for many years. He spent his days thinking and praying. During that time, he made an important discovery. He shared it with us: people and animals, he told us, aren't that different after all. "We only look different," he said. "Inside," he continued, "we are really the same." People, elephants, dogs, bears—each of us can be wise or foolish. Each of us can learn to be great souls, he said. Each of us deserves to be treated with kindness and respect.

Besides the great people we met on our travels, we also met some great bears. One of them was Miggy, a very friendly, calm and amazingly woolly black bear whom we met at a zoo outside Laos's capital city, Vientiane. Both her super-woolly coat and her puffy face were like no other bear's we'd ever seen. Take a look at her photo: surely she had to be a new species, I thought. We plucked some of her hair and sent the sample off to Lisette's lab in Idaho. When the results came back, I was shocked: it showed her DNA was not very different at all from those of other bears in her area!

How could that be? Why, then, did she look so different? Gary has a hypothesis: Miggy's face might be puffy and her coat woolly for the same reason that probably made Goliath, from the First Book of Samuel in the Bible, into a giant. Doctors now know that a defect in the pituitary gland,

a sort of master gland in the brain, can make hair grow thick and bones grow large, especially in the face. No one's ever reported this condition, called *acromegaly,* in a bear before—but maybe both Gary and the monk outside Banglamung are right. Maybe people and bears aren't so different after all!

Our scientific quest continues. Today, Gary is still collecting hairs from bears to fill in the gaps in the mitochondrial map of Cambodia, Laos, and Thailand. Soon he will know what route the moon bears took long ago when they first came south to live in Southeast Asia.

Thailand's Royal Forest Department has officially approved our idea: using our data, with help from the Thai Society for the Conservation of Wild Animals, forest officers are already making plans to release bears from refugee centers like Banglamung into Thailand's empty forests, right back where they came from. Someday soon, the rescued bears will finally go home. We're proud that our work is helping bring that day closer.

Our work isn't always easy. To get our answers, we've needed a wide range of the tools science has to offer—from eyebrow tweezers to whirring machines in a molecular genetics lab. We needed courage to face danger —and the courage to face the possibility we might be wrong. We needed lots of other people to help us, too—from Lisette in her high-tech lab in Idaho to villagers in thatched huts in the Annamite Mountains.

Good thing we were so lucky. Just think of all the happy coincidences that helped make our expedition work: a chance sighting in China over a decade ago. A chance meeting in the Amazon. A lucky introduction at a birthday party. A whim to pluck some hairs from bears we thought we didn't really need.

We hope our luck holds out—because many more important questions lie ahead. Will the bears be safe now, back in their wild homes? How should we monitor their lives to find out? What's the best way to help them remember how to live in the wild? What made the moon bears separate into such different genetic populations? What was the climate like in Southeast Asia 100,000 to 200,000 years ago? How might that have affected moon bears? How can we help Southeast Asian countries protect their forests, their bears, and their human cultures like the Liha and Mo Vang's people? What can we do about the trade in bear gall and other bear parts?

Some of the answers will come from science. Some might arise from chance meetings and lucky coincidence. And some answers may lie in the wisdom of the Buddhist monk's studies or even Mo Vang's book. One thing's for sure: there are surprises in store, and many more mysteries to solve.

And who knows? Maybe some of the answers will come one day from you!

appendices

BEARS BY THE NUMBERS

Number of American black bears alive in the wild: about 750,000

Number of American black bears in lower 48 states: 40,000

Number of brown bears in the wild worldwide: 150,000

Number of polar bears: 20,000–40,000

Number of sloth bears: 7,000–10,000

Number of spectacled bears: about 2,000

Number of pandas left in the wild: about 700

Number of pandas in zoos around the world: about 130

Fraction of the mother's weight that a brown bear cub weighs at birth: 1/720

Fraction of the mother's weight that a human child weighs at birth: 1/20

Number of scientific names used or proposed for the brown or grizzly bear: 86

Running speed of a grizzly: 40 miles per hour

Swimming speed of polar bear: 6 miles per hour

Distance at which a polar bear can smell a seal: 20 miles

Number of calories a black bear can eat in a day: 20,000

Number of hamburgers you'd need to eat a day to get that number of calories: 42

Inches of fat on a polar bear's body: 4

Months a hibernating bear can go without food, drink, or need for a bathroom: 7

Miles a polar bear may travel in a lifetime: 100,000

Home range of a grizzly (in Sweden): 835 square miles

Home range of a giant panda: 1.5–2.5 square miles

Dollars a non-native hunter will pay to hunt a polar bear in Canada: 15,000

Pounds a feasting black bear can gain in one week in the autumn: 30

Potential life span known for most species of bears: 30 years

Average life span of a black bear in northeastern North America, where bear hunting season has reopened: 3 years

LEARN MORE AND HELP BEARS

A number of organizations are working to protect wild bears, rescue captured ones, and protect the wild places where bears and other animals live. Visit their Web pages to learn more; better yet, join one or more of them to help protect bears and forests yourself!

Thai Society for the Conservation of Wild Animals
32 Prathum Cout
85/3-8 Soi Rajaprarop Makkasan
Bangkok, Thailand
www.tscwa.org
TSCWA works with the Thai Royal Forest Department to care for more than a hundred sun and moon bears and hundreds of other animals rescued from poachers, confiscated from illegal owners, or living homeless on the streets. Visit the Web page and you might see pictures of some of the bears you met in this book!

Wildlife Conservation Society
New York Zoological Society
185th St. and Southern Boulevard
Bronx, NY 10460
www.wcs.org
This respected zoo-based organization sponsors wildlife studies and conservation programs in Cambodia, Thailand, and Laos as well as many other countries all over the world. Teams of scientists from WCS were among the first to document many of the new species in Southeast Asia. WCS has worked to establish many protected areas and also fights the illegal use of wild animal body parts for medicine. Visit the Web page and catch up with the latest expeditions.

North American Bear Center
P.O. Box 161
Ely, MN 55731
www.bear.org
Run by bear biologist Dr. Lynn Rogers, the North American Bear Center sponsors studies and conservation projects for American black and grizzly bears. During the winter there is often a live camera in a bear's den, so you can watch mother bears underground with their cubs on your computer!

World Wildlife Fund/TRAFFIC USA
1250 24th St.
Washington, DC 20037
www.wwf.org
World Wildlife Fund is an international organization working in more than forty countries. TRAFFIC USA is its wildlife trade monitoring program. Among its many projects, WWF has sponsored investigations into the Asian trade in bear parts in an effort to stop it. You can order some of these reports from the Web site to learn more.

World Society for the Protection of Animals
29 Perkins St.
Boston, MA 02130
www.wspa-international.org
An international society, WSPA investigates animal cruelty worldwide, including the trade in wild animal parts. It provides critical support for other organizations, including TSCWA and the Banglamung Wildlife Breeding Center, which since our visit has been renamed Banglamung Research Station.

Free the Bears Fund
P.O. Box 673
Mona Vale
New South Wales, Australia
www.freethebears.org.au/savethem/contact_us.html
This organization funded the construction of Mary's Bear Home at Lop Buri Zoo, where Bertha, Dave, and other bears live. The group works to make sure that when bears cannot be released to the wild, their lives are as comfortable and interesting as possible in captivity.

FURTHER READING

For our research in Southeast Asia, Gary, Sun Hean, and I read literally hundreds of books, scientific articles, and newspaper and magazine stories, some of them in languages other than English. You might not want to go that far, but here are just a few books we think you might enjoy.

Animals of Southeast Asia, by Margaret Ayer (New York: St. Martin's Press, 1970).
Bears: Majestic Creatures of the Wild, edited by Ian Stirling (Emmaus, Pa.: Rodale, 1993).
Bears of the World, by Terry Domico (New York: Facts on File, 1988).
The Great American Bear, by Jeff Fair with photographs by Lynn Rogers (Minocqua, Wisc.: Northwood Press, 1990).
The Great Bear Almanac, by Gary Brown (New York: Lyons and Burford, 1993).

Older readers, parents, and teachers might want to read the original book I wrote about our expeditions, which was written for adults:
Search for the Golden Moon Bear: Science and Adventure in Pursuit of a New Species, by Sy Montgomery (New York: Simon and Schuster, 2002).

ACKNOWLEDGMENTS

At a Black Lahu village, a shaman read my fortune. Instead of reading your palm, a shaman in the Black Lahu culture sees your future in the veins of your wrist. "Maybe one person in a thousand has a future like this!" he exclaimed. He had never seen anything like it. He did not foresee wealth for me, or children, or a big house or car. But he saw tremendous luck and great happiness.

Boy, was he right! But I knew that already. For in researching this book, I've been incredibly lucky to have met and worked with wonderful scientists, zookeepers, activists, villagers, scholars, shamans, and bears.

Foremost among them is Dr. Gary Galbreath. No one is more fun to work and travel with, and no one has taught me

so much about evolutionary biology. Meeting Sun Hean in my hometown was just about as amazing as meeting Gary in the Amazon. For this piece of luck I have to thank my friend, conservationist and photographer Eleanor Briggs, who introduced me to Sun Hean. I thank Judith Stout, too, for inviting us all to her birthday party.

Many others helped, too. Our work could never have succeeded without Gary van Zuylen, director of the Thai Society for the Conservation of Wild Animals; Lisette Waits, who sequenced the nucleotides of the DNA we collected and helped interpret the data; and Sangphet Unkeaw, Pranee Thongnoppakun, and Samkait Reinpathomsak, who translated for us when we spoke with local people. Nor could I have completed this book or any other without Dr. A. B. Millmoss, caring for the animals at home.

For help in producing this book for children, I thank consultants Selinda Chiquoine and Robert and Judith Oksner; photographer Dianne T. L. Taylor-Snow; organizational genius Joni Praded; photo researcher Ned Lee; my literary agent, Sarah Jane Freymann; and my editor at Houghton Mifflin, Kate O'Sullivan.

Finally, our project certainly would not have worked without the bears' cooperation! I would thank them all by name here—except that they would really rather eat a marshmallow.

A NOTE ABOUT OUR IMAGES

The photos in this book are very special. They are the only photos of golden moon bears in the world, to our knowledge —certainly they are the only photos known to science. Gary and I took photos of the bears while we were pulling out hairs

and taking other data. Sometimes our scientific friends and helpers—Heng Kimmchay and Dianne Taylor-Snow—took photos for us. But never did any of us get to use fancy lights or camera lenses. So our photos don't look like formal portraits from a photo studio—they were snapped in the field.